Bright SPARKS!

Contents

Zoo News
Written by Paul Bright and illustrated by Alice Brereton 2

Volcano Alert!
Written by Christine Taylor-Butler 6

When You Were My Age
Written by Paul Bright and illustrated by Mike Redman 12

King Kafu and the Seasons
Written by Trish Cooke and illustrated by Andrea Castellani 16

Can You Change the World?
Written by Libby Martinez 22

Not A Word
Written by Cary Fagan and illustrated by Kevin Myers 28

When the Lights Went Out
Written by Bill Nagelkerke and illustrated by Alex Lopez 34

Zoo News

by Paul Bright

This is Zak the zoo-keeper.
Oh, how he loves to talk!
He chats to all the animals,
Who growl or grunt or squawk,
But little does he realise
That every beast and bird
Is passing on the things he says –
Or what they think they've heard.

Keeper Zak made breakfast
For the spiders, sharks and skinks,
And cut some juicy beef-steak
For the leopard and the lynx.
Then, feeding the koalas
From the eucalyptus tree,
He said: "Is that the time?
I think I'll make a cup of tea."

Make a cup of tea?

Lion said to Bear, "He thinks
He'll shake a chimpanzee."
Then Bear told Penguin, "Wow!
The skunk and snake are on TV!"
Penguin said to Seal, "He says
He'll take me home to ski."
Seal said, "How bizarre –
Zak's having cake with mushy peas."

Keeper Zak cleaned out the goats,
Gorilla and giraffe;
He fed the capybara,
Heard the kookaburra laugh.
He picked up lots of litter,
And the gum some people chew.
Then he said, "I'll stop and have
My snack at half past two."

Snack at half past two?

Warthog said to Polar Bear,
"He smacked the kangaroo!"
Polar Bear told Bat, "He's sent
The yak to Timbuktu!"
Then Bat told Rat, "He said
He heard the kakapo say 'moo'!"
Rat replied, "What did you say?
A quacking cockatoo?"

I must go home to eat, thought Zak.
It's getting rather late.
Perhaps I'll have a pizza,
Or some pasta on a plate.
Keeper Zak packed up his tools
And locked them in his shed –
And called a farewell greeting
As he cycled home to bed.

But what was that he said?

Ostrich called to Owl, "He said,
'It's time for bed – goodnight!'"
Crocodile told Caiman,
"He said, 'Everyone sleep tight.'"
Then Terrapin told Tortoise,
"He said, 'Mind the bugs don't bite.'"

And, of course,
    They all
        Were right.

Amazing Animals

Zak looks after lots of exotic animals. Do you know all of them? Can you spot these animals in the pictures?

Capybaras are like very large guinea pigs. They come from South America and love to swim.

Caimans are very similar to alligators. They come from Central and South America.

Kakapos are large, yellowish-green parrots from New Zealand. They're so big that they can't fly!

Kookaburras are a type of kingfisher bird from Australia. Their calls sound like laughter.

Skinks are lizards, but they look a lot like snakes! They have little or no legs and don't have clear necks.

Yaks are large cows from Central Asia. They have long, curly hair and can weigh up to 1000 kg.

Volcano Alert!

by Christine Taylor-Butler

What is a volcano?

A volcano is a large opening in Earth's surface. Earth's heat and gases escape from this large opening. Beneath Earth's surface, pressure and heat build up. This melts the rock and minerals. The **molten** hot rock is called **magma**. Magma escapes to the surface when a volcano erupts. When magma flows out of a volcano, it is called **lava**. Lava is dangerously hot.

lava

Most volcanoes form over thousands of years.

Did you know?

- Jupiter's moon Io has more active volcanoes than Earth.
- The tallest volcano in the solar system is on Mars.
- The islands of Hawaii are the tops of ocean volcanoes.

Io is slightly larger than Earth's moon and covered with hundreds of volcanoes.

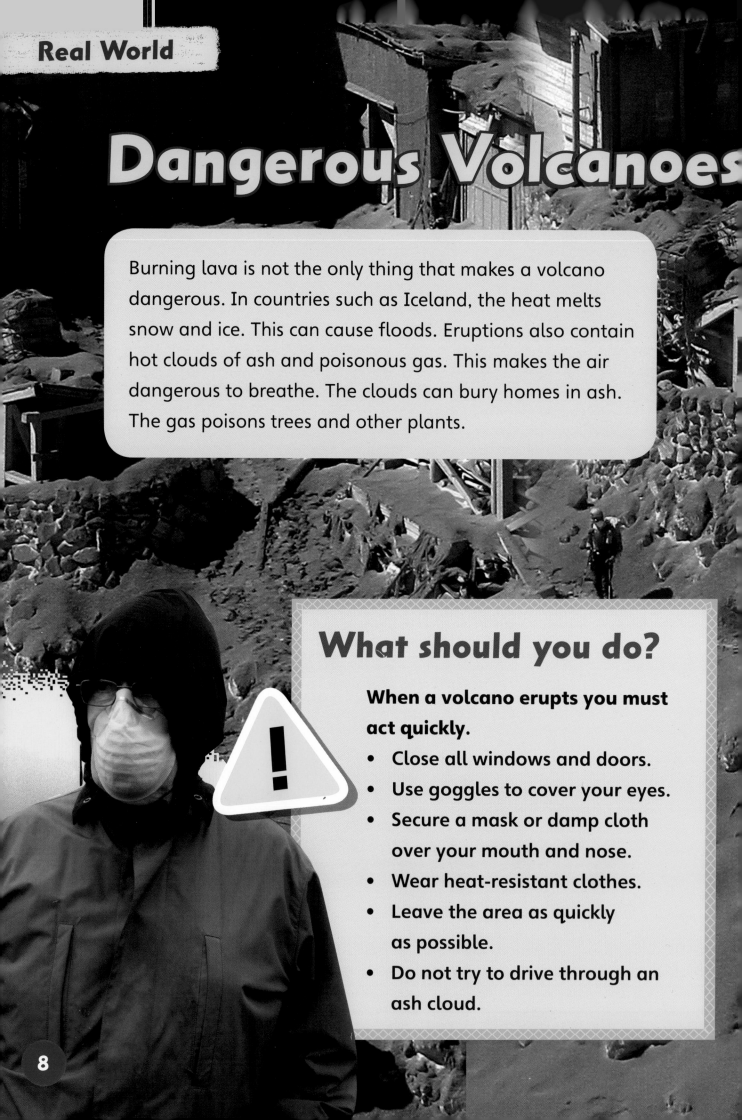

Dangerous Volcanoes

Burning lava is not the only thing that makes a volcano dangerous. In countries such as Iceland, the heat melts snow and ice. This can cause floods. Eruptions also contain hot clouds of ash and poisonous gas. This makes the air dangerous to breathe. The clouds can bury homes in ash. The gas poisons trees and other plants.

What should you do?

When a volcano erupts you must act quickly.

- **Close all windows and doors.**
- **Use goggles to cover your eyes.**
- **Secure a mask or damp cloth over your mouth and nose.**
- **Wear heat-resistant clothes.**
- **Leave the area as quickly as possible.**
- **Do not try to drive through an ash cloud.**

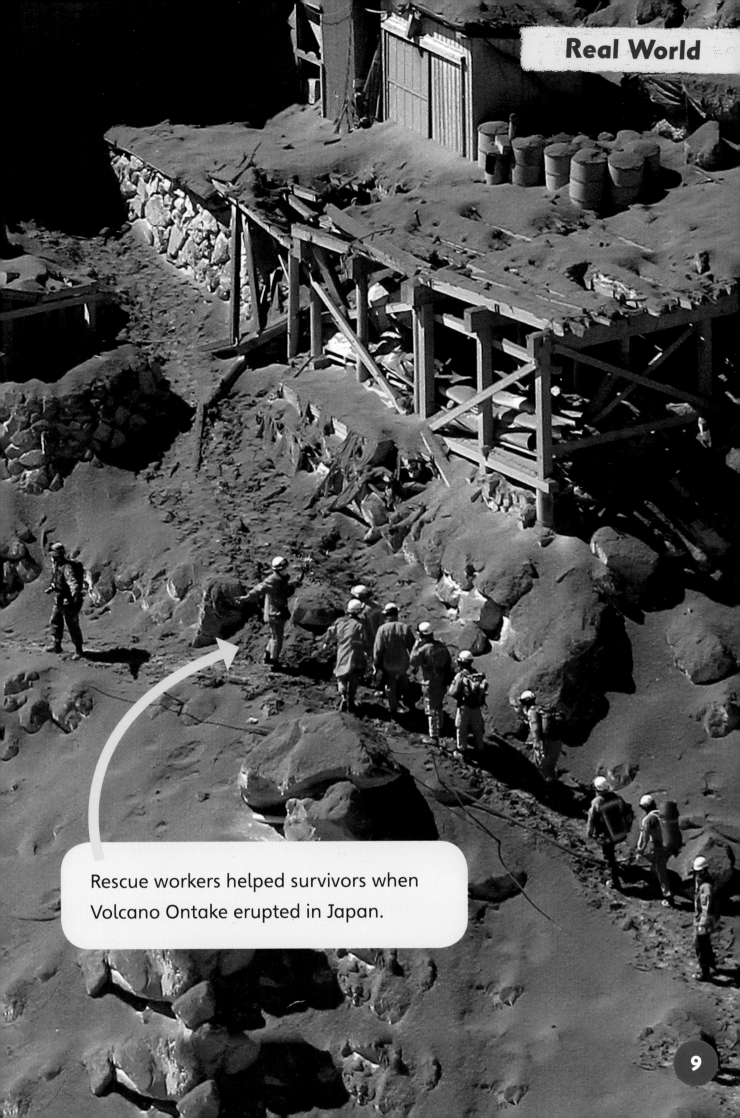

Rescue workers helped survivors when Volcano Ontake erupted in Japan.

Understanding Volcanoes

Many volcanoes are dormant. This means they are not erupting, but they could erupt in the future. Some volcanoes are extinct. This means they are not likely to erupt.

JOB PROFILE

Scientists who study volcanoes are called volcanologists. Their jobs are dangerous. They measure a volcano's temperature and collect samples. They wear special protective clothing. The information they collect is used to predict when a volcano will erupt. It also helps scientists understand why eruptions happen.

FACT FILE

A volcano erupted in Iceland on 20th March 2010. By 14th April, the ash cloud rose over 10 kilometres into the air. It damaged aeroplane engines. Airline travel in Europe was stopped for seven days.

Glossary

lava magma that flows out of a volcano

magma liquid rock that is under the ground

molten so hot that it has become liquid

When You Were My Age

by Paul Bright

"Happy birthday, Grandpa! Can you tell – I'd love to know:
What was it like when you were small, a long, long time ago?"

Grandpa thought, and said, "I know a way to make this fun.
You ask me lots of questions, and I'll answer every one.
Most of what I tell you will be absolutely true …
But sometimes I might tell a fib: just one or maybe two!"

"So Grandpa, Grandpa, tell me – my first question of all:
Was your house much like mine is, when you were only small?"

"Our living room was warm and snug, the coal fire glowing red,
But, oh, the winter goosebump chill when we went up to bed!
There was ice inside the windows, and chilly morning air.
We'd rush to pull on pants and vests, and scurry down the stairs."

"Now Grandpa, Grandpa, tell me – I really want to know:
Did you have a mobile phone, a long, long time ago?"

"A phone? You must be joking! No, we had no phone at all,
Just a call-box down the road: red and square and tall.
Two silver buttons, 'A' and 'B', were pressed by every kid,
To find the pennies left behind – although I never did."

"But did you have a TV, when you were eight or nine?
What was your favourite programme? Bet it's not the same as mine!"

"My dad brought home a TV when I was, maybe, five.
You should have heard me cheering on the day that it arrived!
The picture was in black and white, and really, really small –
But there were lots of cowboy films, I liked those most of all."

"Were you given pocket money? More than me, I bet!
When you were just as old as me, how much did you get?"

"I think I got two shillings, or maybe half a crown.
Yes, money then was different – I can see that made you frown.
Tuppence bought a comic or a chunky chocolate bar,
Or maybe sherbet lemons from the sweet shop's big glass jar."

"Did you have a gerbil, or a budgie in a cage?
Grandpa, did you have a pet, when you were just my age?"

"Of all our cats and rats and birds, the one I thought was best,
Was Dorothy the dodo, who'd fallen from her nest.
I fed her dates and doughnuts, and chewy chocolate mints,
Until one day she flew away – I haven't seen her since."

"There's still another question – I thought it might be fun:
What sounds do you remember that you heard when you were young?"

"Whistling Bill, the milkman: he had a horse and cart.
The horse knew all the houses, where to stop and where to start.
We'd hear the bottles clinking as he took them from the crate,
So 'clip-clop', 'clink-clunk', whistling and the creaking of the gate."

"Now, here's my final question – the very last of all:
Grandpa, were there dinosaurs when you were really small?"

"Now you're getting cheeky! What a sneaky joke to make!
Did I blow out 100 million candles on my cake?
I may be grey and wrinkled, but I don't feel old at all.
Now put your jacket on. I'll race you all the way to school!"

Grandpa says that's how it was, when he was young, like you –
But are there any naughty fibs? Can you say what's true?

TELEPHONE

Hello?

To make a call from a public phone box, you had to put in coins and then dial the number. If someone answered, you pressed button 'A' so they could hear you. If no-one answered, you pressed button 'B' to get your money back.

King Kafu and the Seasons
by Trish Cooke

Part 1

Long ago in a far-off land, in a tiny village, there lived a king. His name was Kafu. King Kafu loved to eat, and King Kafu's chef loved to cook tasty dishes for him.

One day, as Chef strolled around the palace gardens, he noticed some bushes he hadn't seen before. The bushes were full of colourful berries.

When Chef looked in his recipe book, he saw that these strange fruits were called pockle-berries. Chef baked the pockle-berries in a tart and took it to the king.

"Ooooooh – this tart is the best tart I have ever tasted!" said King Kafu. "From now on, you must make pockle-berry tart for me every day!"

However, one chilly morning in early autumn, Chef got a terrible shock. He went out into the palace gardens to pick more pockle-berries, but there were no more berries on the bushes!

Chef went back into the palace to tell the king.

"King Kafu," said Chef, "I'm afraid I can't make you any more pockle-berry tarts. You see, winter is coming. The pockle-berries grow only in summer …"

"Nonsense!" cried King Kafu. "You must find some!"

Chef didn't know what to do.

"The king wants a pockle-berry tart, but there are no more pockle-berries on the bushes. What am I to do?" he asked the kitchen maid.

"Pockle-berries don't grow when it's cold," the kitchen maid said. "It's winter here, so we'll have to go somewhere warmer to find some."

"Brilliant idea!" said Chef.

17

The next morning, Chef and
the maid set out on their travels.
They travelled far and wide,
through snow and blizzard,
through rain and storm,
for days and months.
Finally, Chef and the maid reached a place
where the sun was shining and there were
fields and fields of pockle-berry bushes.

Part 2

Chef and the kitchen maid quickly picked as many pockle-berries as they could carry. Then they packed the berries in their bags and set off for home.

Once again, they travelled for days and months,
    through storm and rain
        and blizzard and snow,
            until they arrived back at the palace.

The king greeted them in the palace gardens, where once again the sun was shining and the air was warm.

"I now have the pockle-berries, Your Majesty!" said Chef. "I will make you your pockle-berry tart right away!"

"About time," said a grumpy King Kafu.

But, as Chef and the maid opened their bags, King Kafu cried out, "These pockle-berries are ROTTEN!"

The journey had taken so long that the berries had turned bad.

"What about my pockle-berry tart?" said King Kafu, sadly.

Just then, the kitchen maid looked up.

"Look!" she said excitedly. "The pockle-berry bushes here at the palace have berries on them again! We were gone so long that the seasons changed!"

Chef and the maid rushed to pick all the berries off the bushes.

King Kafu was happy, but Chef looked sad.

"What's wrong?" the maid asked.

"These berries will grow only while it's summer," said Chef. "What will I do in winter?"

The maid smiled. "I have an idea," she said.

In the kitchen, the maid set to work. She put some of the pockle-berries in a pan and poured in some sugar. She stirred and stirred, until the berries turned gooey and sticky. They looked delicious.

"What are you doing?" said Chef.

"I'm making pockle-berry jam!" said the maid. "The fruit won't last very long – but, when we make it into jam, it lasts for a long, long time! You can use the jam to make the king's tarts in winter."

"That's brilliant!" said Chef, happily. "We can make pockle-berry tarts for the king all year long!"

So, that is exactly what Chef did. King Kafu was delighted.

As for the maid – well, she soon became a chef too, making the best jam the village had ever tasted!

Can You Change the World?

by Libby Martinez

Young people around the world are solving problems to make their neighbourhoods better. Let's meet one of them!

FACT FILE

Kelvin Doe
Age: 18 years old
Home town: Freetown, Sierra Leone

Kelvin Doe is an inventor. He taught himself how to make things! When Kelvin was ten years old, he decided he wanted to help people. He started to think of ideas. Kelvin thought about problems in his neighbourhood. There was a lack of electricity and the lights came on only once a week. Kelvin had an idea to help the lights stay on!

SIERRA LEONE

FREETOWN

FACT FILE

Sierra Leone

Location: Sierra Leone is a country in West Africa.
Population: More than five million people
Capital: Freetown
Climate: Tropical

Power Up!

Lights on!

Kelvin's family could not afford batteries, and the lights needed batteries to work. Kelvin wanted to fix the problem. When he was thirteen years old, he started collecting electronic parts that people had thrown away and used the parts to make a battery. Now Kelvin's batteries power lights all over his neighbourhood!

Mobile phone power

Kelvin kept thinking of ideas to help. His next invention was a **generator**. It charged batteries. His neighbours needed these batteries to charge their mobile phones.

Did You Know?

More than 1.3 billion people have no electricity. That's more than 20 times the number of people who live in the United Kingdom!

What's Next?

Future plans

Kelvin keeps inventing and working on ideas. One of his new projects is building a windmill. The windmill will provide power to his neighbourhood. He is also working on a **solar power** project to power computers. Students will be able to use these computers to go on the internet.

Solar panels collect energy from the Sun. The energy is used to make electricity.

Glossary

climate type of weather a place usually has

generator machine that can produce electrical energy

solar power energy from the Sun that is converted into electricity

These children are using old packaging to make a bird feeder.

WHAT CAN YOU DO?

Be creative, like Kelvin! Reuse items to help solve problems. You could use plastic bottles to make bird feeders. This would help wildlife in your neighbourhood.

Not A Word

by Cary Fagan

Part 1

"We could walk backwards, balancing eggs on our heads!" I said. Emily laughed. She sits next to me at school.

"We don't want to waste eggs," Ms Kasana said. "Think: we need a challenge to complete inside for an hour, as a fundraiser. If we do it, the supermarket will donate a hundred pounds' worth of food to the food bank."

"What's a food bank?" asked Jing Fei.

Harvey grinned. "It's where you deposit vegetables."

Harvey thought he was being funny. I knew, though, that last year Emily's dad lost his job and her mum got ill, and they needed to use the food bank for three months.

Ms Kasana said, "Every day, people in our own community go hungry. The food bank distributes food to people in need – and I think we should do our part. Someone must have an idea."

Emily put up her hand. "We could have a sponsored silence. Nobody speaks – not even you, Miss. Not even Lewis!"

"Me? What do you mean?" I asked. "I could go two weeks without talking!"

Ms Kasana smiled. "Great idea, Emily." Inside, I groaned.

◇◇◇◇◇◇◇◇◇◇◇◇◇◇◇◇◇◇◇◇◇◇◇◇

That was a week ago.

Now, until break time, nobody could say a word.

"There'll be no passing notes, either," said Ms Kasana. "I'll write your work on the whiteboard. Everyone ready?"

We all nodded. "All right," said Ms Kasana. "We'll start … now!" Ms Kasana wrote: "Science projects". My favourite subject!

Everybody in class had a project: Harvey was growing sunflowers; Emily was taking care of a mouse; Jing Fei was making up healthy recipes. I was designing a space station, and I knew just what I was going to add next. Then my pencil's tip snapped.

"Em–" I began, but then remembered not to talk. I tapped her arm and held up my pencil.

She squinted at me, meaning, *What?* I pretended to write, and then looked in surprise at the pencil. I saw realisation dawn on Emily's face. She gave me her sharpener.

As I walked to the bin, Emily went to the cage on the windowsill. Today, she was trying out different foods on the mouse: she put in some raisins, and came back. Then I turned towards the window and almost shouted out.

The cage door was open!

SCIENCE PROJECTS

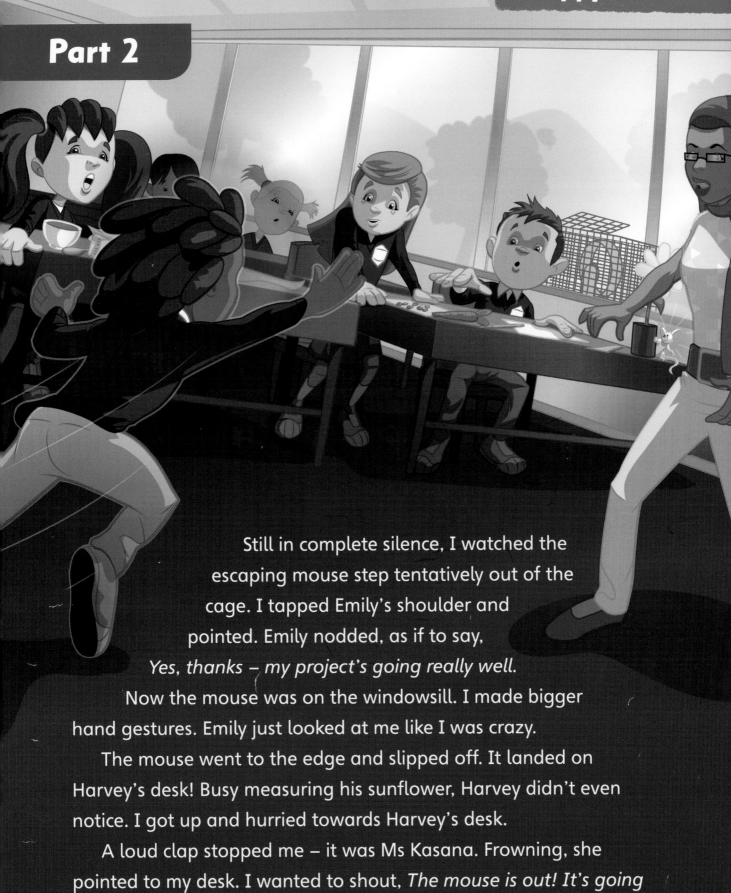

Still in complete silence, I watched the escaping mouse step tentatively out of the cage. I tapped Emily's shoulder and pointed. Emily nodded, as if to say, *Yes, thanks – my project's going really well.*

Now the mouse was on the windowsill. I made bigger hand gestures. Emily just looked at me like I was crazy.

The mouse went to the edge and slipped off. It landed on Harvey's desk! Busy measuring his sunflower, Harvey didn't even notice. I got up and hurried towards Harvey's desk.

A loud clap stopped me – it was Ms Kasana. Frowning, she pointed to my desk. I wanted to shout, *The mouse is out! It's going to get lost, or hurt!* But, if I spoke, I knew we'd lose the money for the food bank.

I had a choice. I could lose the money or I could get into trouble. I decided to get into trouble.

The mouse was sliding down the leg of Harvey's desk. I dove towards it. I missed.

Everyone jumped out of my way as I crashed into chairs and bookshelves. I scrambled to my feet looking around desperately, and then ran up the aisle between the desks, after the mouse. It hopped onto some books and then onto Ms Kasana's desk.

I lunged at the mouse, but *it* jumped, too – right onto my head!

I had no choice: I had to trap the mouse while I knew where it was.

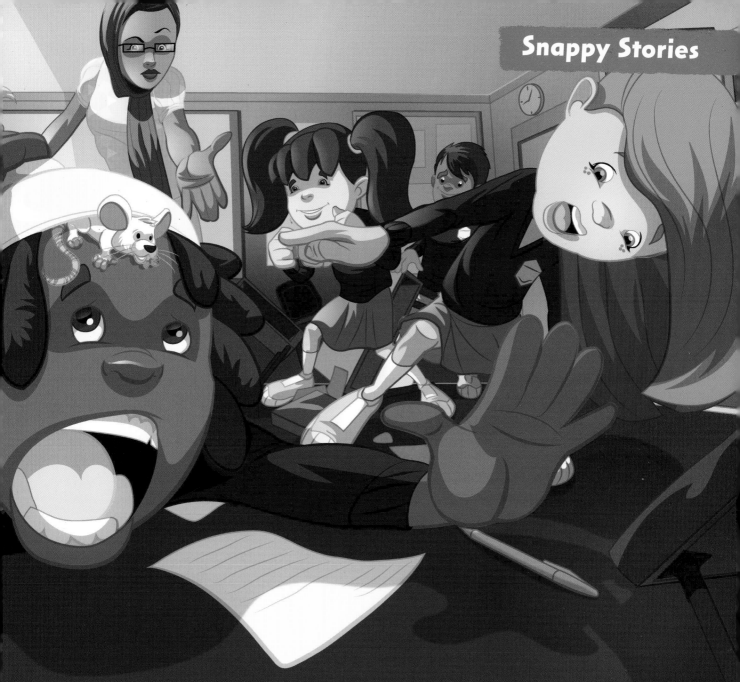

I looked around and saw Jing Fei's cooking stuff. I picked up a plastic bowl and put it, upside down, on my head.

The whole class had now gathered around me. They were trying not to laugh. Ms Kasana glared. She held out her hand.

What could I do? I lifted up the bowl. I could feel the mouse stand up on my head. Everyone's eyes grew wide, including Ms Kasana's.

Emily carefully picked the mouse off my head. She put it back into the cage. Firmly, she latched the door – and then turned around and smiled at me.

Ms Kasana smiled at me, too. We went back to our desks. I didn't say a word until break time ... but I had an awful lot to say after that!

When the Lights Went Out
by Bill Nagelkerke

Part 1

The night was dark and stormy.

Wind howled and sleet fell.

Alex was busy with homework. Bella was finishing one of her stories. Dad was in the kitchen, making soup.

"We'll eat as soon as Mum gets home," he said. "Piping hot soup will be exactly what she needs."

Then Bella screeched. "My screen just turned off!"

The lights went off as well.

"What's happening?" Alex asked the darkness.

"Looks like a power cut," Dad answered. "You two stay where you are." They heard him scrabbling around in the kitchen.

"I can't find any candles!" he called.

"They're under the sink," Bella called back. "With some matches – and there's a torch as well."

"Got them," said Dad, sighing with relief.

He lit the candles carefully. The room became filled with enormous, dancing shadows.

"The whole street's dark," said Dad, peering outside.

"Let's pretend it's a little bit exciting," said Bella.

"I'm starting to feel cold," Alex shivered.

"That's because the heating went off as well," Dad said. "I'm sure it'll be fixed soon."

"What if it isn't?" said Alex, sounding suddenly panic-stricken. "Some of the kids were talking at school."

"About what?" asked Dad.

"About *everyone* running out of power!"

"Our teacher said it *could* happen, if the winter was extra cold," agreed Bella.

"I heard something like that on the news," Dad admitted, "but I didn't really believe it."

"What if it's run out tonight?" said Alex.

"It can't have run out just like that ..." said Dad. "Can it?"

He held his watch under a candle flame. "It's nearly news time ... but the TV won't work."

"We've got a battery radio," said Bella. "It's in the hall cupboard."

"Well remembered!" said Dad. "I'll get it."

"I'm not excited," Alex whispered to Bella. "I'm scared."

Bella nodded. "Me too – a bit."

"And I'm hungry," grumbled Alex.

"I hope this works," said Dad, coming back with the radio – and a banana for each of them.

"I put in new batteries last week," said Bella. "In the torch, as well."

"You've thought of everything," said Dad, sounding like he was smiling at her.

"Our teacher said to be prepared," said Bella. "Just in case."

Dad turned the dial and found a news programme just starting. They all crossed their fingers.

Part 2

Bella, Alex and their dad listened, and waited, as the newsreaders spoke. Finally, the news finished – and they had said nothing at all about the power cut.

"That's a relief!" said Dad. "The power can't be off everywhere."

"But it's still off here," said Bella. "I hope old Mr Starek next door is okay."

"I'll check on him when Mum gets home," said Dad.

"Let's give her a call," said Bella.

The landline wasn't working, but Dad's mobile was.

"Good thing I charged it," he said, dialling and holding it to his ear. "No answer. It's going straight to voicemail."

"That's good," said Bella. "It means that Mum's driving."

Alex shivered again.

"Let's try to keep warm," said Dad.

The three of them squashed up on the sofa, under a thick, woolly blanket.

"What now?" asked Alex.

"How about a story?" Bella suggested.

"It's way too dark to read!" said Alex.

"Not reading: *telling*," said Bella. "I'll tell you my latest one!"

Bella began telling her tale into the darkness. Soon, Alex and Dad were spellbound. The story was so good that none of them even heard Mum come home.

"Where is everyone?" she called.

"We're in here," Dad called back, beaming the torch into the doorway.

"All okay?" Mum asked. "Sorry I'm late: I stopped to talk to some power-company workers. The wind's brought down several lines – that's why there's no power. They said it shouldn't be too long before everything's working again. What a stormy night!"

"It's a *story* night as well!" said Bella. "Come and hear the end of it."

Mum joined them all under the blanket.

When Bella finished, they all stayed sitting still for a minute, getting used to the real world again. Dad gave Bella's hand a squeeze.

"I'll visit Mr Starek," he said then, standing and taking the torch. "I'll see if he'd rather come over here."

"Well, it could have been a lot worse," said Alex.

"I thought you liked it!" Bella replied, sounding offended.

"I meant the power cut!" Alex reassured her. "What do we do if it *is* worse next time?"

"Be even better prepared, I suppose," Bella said.

"That's all we can do," agreed Mum.

"That, *and* have more stories to tell!" grinned Bella.

Published by Pearson Education Limited, 80 Strand, London, WC2R 0RL.

www.pearsonschools.co.uk

Text © Pearson Education Limited 2016
Original illustrations © Pearson Education Limited 2016

Illustrated by Andrea Castellani, Alice Brereton, Mike Redman, Kevin Myers and Alex Lopez

First published 2016

20 19 18
10 9 8 7 6 5 4

British Library Cataloguing in Publication Data
A catalogue record for this book is available from the British Library

ISBN 978 0 435 17968 7

Printed in the UK by Ashford Colour Press

Acknowledgements
The publisher would like to thank the following individuals and organisations for their kind permission to reproduce their photographs:

(Key: b-bottom; c-center; l-left; r-right; t-top)

6-7 Alamy Images: Westend61 GmbH. **7 Alamy Images:** Westend61 GmbH (t); Stocktrek Images, Inc (b). **8-9 Getty Images:** JIJI PRESS / AFP. **8 Alamy Images:** Bjarki Reyr EYJ (bl). **10 Alamy Images:** Rafael Ben-Ari (bl). **Getty Images:** HALLDOR KOLBEINS / AFP (c). **10-11 Alamy Images:** Stocktrek Images, Inc. **22-23 Alamy Images:** Fabian von Poser. **22 Getty Images:** John Lamparski / Wireimage. **23 Alamy Images:** Peter Hermes Furian. **24-25 Alamy Images:** Bernhard Classen. **24 Alamy Images:** Lee Karen Stow. **25 Alamy Images:** Charles Sturge. **26-27 Alamy Images:** Blend Images. **27 Alamy Images:** Wenn Ltd

Cover images: *Front:* **Alamy Images:** Rafael Ben-Ari

All other images © Pearson Education